wrong turn to creek street

Russell Peter

Presentation by *BookLeaf Publishing*

Web: www.bookleafpub.com

E-mail: info@bookleafpub.com

ISBN: 9789357441520

First edition 2023

one

want badly to be not what we are
we are where we would rather not be
what we're doing is not what we want to do
keep going places we never thought we'd go
surprised to be seeing what we'd see
never knowing why we don't seem to know
how we came to have things we don't need
feeding bad habits that shouldn't be fed
never wanting to get out of bed
who we should be and what we once were
don't know who he is, don't recognize her
when we'll stop growing, for how long we'll
grow
pray we start knowing the things we don't know

two

the adult tree in the back driveway that slopes
down to the swamp
where the trees were lined up respectively in the
marsh below each house
the adult tree that belonged to me with the hole
upon its chest
through which i'd climb until one day i got
caught at my breast
i must have grown since yesterday
i must have gained some weight
i cannot get past my shoulders
can't make it through the gate
i peer into the opening , and barely see the doors
can't see beyond the halls that lead to tunnels
underground
no one knows the stories that lay hidden beneath
the ground
in secret pockets buried full of wonderous deceit
unbeknownst to anyone miles below our feet
magic worlds of wonder through the portal in
the tree
memories from within his room that only i can
see

three

What a service she provides
The woman with child
Trying harder than I should to empathize
With something I don't recognize
They no longer have a look or type
And when you look between her thighs
You can just make out her vulva
No this mother is not the same
As the ideals they've forced upon us
She makes eye contact with me while holding
her naked breast
In her hand in broad daylight at my favorite cafe
downtown
Daring onlookers not to look
Cramming a sore dry teat into the mouth of an
unwilling toddler
Demanding my respect

four

knowing right from wrong somehow
never stopped me doing what i want
never going to stop and just be
happy with what i've got
there'll always be something someplace
the thought of someone else
that lures me out from safety
into someone else's mess
always going to be a thing
somewhere yonder that i'll want
always going to get to have
a shit more than i've got
things i have are not enough
there's more shit i could get
and so i'll keep on getting shit
you thought i'd never get
i'll keep on getting shit forever
never gonna stop
never going to be ok
with just the stuff i've got

five

name a place more safe than right here in my
bed
where every night i lay to rest my tired aching
head
nothing out there in the world will keep me from
my bed
no where in the world at night i'd rather be
instead
sucked into a wormhole of blackness in my bed
defying space and gravity beneath the damp
bedspread
musky dank and humid i am both naked and
warm
here where you are rough with me but never do
me harm
no other place in the world that defies time and
space
here when im on top and then i look down at
your face
where minutes turn to hours and the nights turn
into days
repositioning our bodies in a hundred thousand
ways
here where so much time goes by cradling my
head

the place where i retreat each night to wallow in
my dread

6

six

7

It can't be wrong if you're having fun
why feel guilt for feeling pleasure
The moments that pass are already gone
Revel in pleasure from wherever it comes
Never apologize to anyone
Especially when you've had such fun
Think of all the stuff you've done
to be all that you have become
Don't feel bad for having fun
You deserve pleasure more than anyone

seven

Tiptoeing a thin line between fantasy and
obsession
Bogged down by a brain fog stifling what
matters most
And illuminating somehow in its gloom
Any possibility that you might still be
Thinking about me
feeling like i'm in control but losing my
discretion
drowning out the sounds of all the things that are
important
And somehow glowing in the dark
Is the fleeting hope that you might still be
Thinking about me

eight

indulge in all of what there is
take whatever comes your way
Why choose between this or that
why just have one when you can have two
there's nothing wrong with wanting more
its okay to entertain thoughts about
the things we can't do
it's only human to want to ravage you
so long as i don't act
or let you know i think of you
and that's how we respect
people, by not telling them what we think
and so we can indulge in thoughts
we aren't supposed to think
so long as i should never share
what i feel for you
indulge in all the secret lust
when i should dream of you

nine

i am free to speak my truth
unless i'm being polite
For politeness is the marker of a good girl
who stifles their opinions for the sake of your
feelings
when your fragility takes precedent to truth
this is politeness
Who cares what I think if you feel good
Who cares that I hate what makes you feel good
Who cares that I lie to make you feel good
I will stifle my truth just so you can feel good
Because that's how a good polite girl should

ten

someone who has no time for girlfriends
Who just wants to cuddle
And give relationship advice
someone who just wants to give
Long deep tissue massages
And spoon me softly to sleep
someone who wants nothing
But to eat me out
And leave promptly after I cum
if i could put this on tinder
then i surely would
someone who lets me go home to my man
and is happy to see me whenever he can
and has eyes for no one except for me
and is only there for me when i need
if i could put this on tinder then i would indeed

eleven

doesn't want me to get too close
but really likes to feel my throat
doesn't let me stay too long
but wonders if i'll swallow
pulls off my clothes real fast
then needs me to leave
clings onto my hips urgently
and asks to drive me home
doesn't really care too much
but feels that i should know
he's here for me whenever
i should wanna have a go
climbs up to my shoulders
cushioning my head
asks me for my throat again
then wants to go to bed
tells me that its only sex
hes just a friend that grabs my neck
grabs me all the clothes i own
offers to drive me home
atleast will walk me to the door
invites me back if i want more

twelve

13

the selfie is
a divine act of femininity
of womb-deep urgency
from the galaxy i've seen
drawn within the vulvas
i've seen on the internet
by digital artists, derived
from intuition and magic
and creation
curated depictions
of who i wish i could be
exactly as i need to be seen
especially by those
who've never seen me
its them who i need
to see this dear me
the feminine urge
to show them a me
that's barely the me
anyone has seen
the capture is witchcraft
that shows you the me
that i want you to see

thirteen

snuggle entrapment, abusing addiction to skin on
skin contact
narcotic dependence on body snuggling
skin-on-skin pressing face to neck front to back
chest to chest hypnotization
fingers interlocked around necks
suffocating by loving embrace
filling my lungs with your breath
sniffing the skin across your face
tracing shoulders with our lips
holding you against your will
hands wrapped around my wrists
the only way to give you love
is to pass it through my skin
bring you so close i can feel you from within
addicted to the way it tastes
the feeling when you grab my waist
make you depend on my love
make sure im who you're dreaming of

fourteen

15

the air is unseasonably warm
the dog is unreasonably stiff
and sadness permeates the old bones
because this is what happens now
when the pressure drops
this tragic arrangement of admissions of guilt
heartbreaking turmoil of secrets
churning in the pit of my soul
swirling in the madness of stories untold
secret betrayals never revealed
and the darkness that inevitably unfolds
letting the guilt mature like wine
in a cellar where the dark resides
swept under the rug where no one will look
eloquently arranged in the guise of a book

fifteen

typing girl boasts confidence from screens she
hides behind
talking girl is too concerned with what is on
their minds
talking girl trips over words when she is trying
to speak
typing girl came up with this shit while you were
half asleep
type the thoughts instead of talk when talking is
insane
talking words and typing words is somehow not
the same
a different girl that types the words
than the one that does the speaking
they're both the same but the one that writes
is the one that is worth keeping
the girl that talks says things a lot
says things that never happen
the girl that writes makes you believe
that anything can happen
typing girl makes you laugh when you read
talking girl isn't quite what you need

sixteen

suddenly you will emerge from the chaos of
existence
if everything is up in flames and you decide not
to burn
then from the ashes you will rise unbothered by
the flames
despite the foreground burning up time and time
again
this is the way with life sometimes, love burns
down to the ground
so often does it set ablaze the bounty that you've
found
that suddenly should you emerge from chaos
with understanding
and a feeling of persistence pushing through
smoke of failures
and ill will and come out on the other side a
better version still
if everything came crumbling down who'd you
love most? where are they now
when everything burns and nothing's left and
there you are beside yourself
suddenly you will determine which direction
you will turn in

the slightest left turn to dark and sorrow but rest
your head and look tomorrow
back at the chaos of fires you set one last time
before moving ahead

seventeen

hooked on patterns we didn't mean to create
depending on customs we really should break
we know in our hearts we shouldn't repeat
mistakes that we made while we were in heat
and you know looking back you should never
have let
me walk up your driveway and into your bed
now we count down the days till the moons in
the sky
to see which one of us sits idly by
while the other lies awake plotting hundreds of
ways
to tempt the other to make a mistake

eighteen

i feel most compelled to do something
when i really should do nothing
i cannot help but feel the need to do something
when doing something could ruin everything
when everyone would be better of knowing
nothing
i feel they deserve to know something
i always feel the need to have to tell you
something
im always going to want to have a thing to say
how much time should go by before i say
something
trying to find a reason to have to tell you
something
making up a reason that i'd need to show you
something

nineteen

keep an eye when she's distracted
wonder where she goes
watch her when you fall asleep
she's always good to go
slips out the back when you don't watch
clambers out the windows
make sure he never knows you call
and she'll be good to go
know that when you doubt her
it probably goes to show
she covers up the footprints that
she tracked across the snow
watch how when you go to bed
she slips out the back door
you'd never know she got around
that she's a little whore
she'll slip back in without a sound
and love you to your core
won't dare to try her luck again
until she wants some more

twenty

yearning to be touched by you
remembering how it felt
feeling the dumb way it hurts
hoping that it ends
wondering if i'll ever
get to see you again
holding on to words
spoken way back when
knowing that you wont
want this in the end
feeling how it hurts
want to be your friend
anything to get you
to see me once again
yearning for your touch
remember how it felt
hearing whispered words
i never share with friends
wondering if i'll ever
see your face again
knowing that you'd never
want me in the end

twenty one

flashing back to images of my face in your
hands
my stomach drops right through the floor
and i can barely stand
flashback to you asking without words to grip
my neck
trying to mind my business and suddenly i gasp
as im teleported to looking up from between
your thighs
shameful i do not have the courage to meet your
eyes
can't unsee the spit strings after all this time's
gone by
can still feel how you pushed it all the way that
it could go
remember how you hesitated when you heard
me choke
just trying to mind my business when i flashback
to a time
that supposedly never happened but is always on
my mind